Reinaldo Domingos

In a Sustainable World

1st Edition

About the series

The series "Money Boy" is a children's adaptation based upon the DSOP Financial Education Methodology, conceived by master, professor, educator, and financial therapist Reinaldo Domingos.

The series is part of the DSOP Financial Education Program that ranges from grammar school to college. It consists of 30 didactic volumes (15 textbooks and 15 teacher's books) and six paradidactic volumes that comprise subjects of family, diversity, sustainability, autonomy, and citizenship.

In addition to the books, the schools that adopt the DSOP Financial Education Program are entitled to pedagogical training, financial education workshops for teachers, lectures for the students and the community, and access to the school website (portalescolas.dsop.com.br), which consists of class plans, interactive activities (games), videos, and exclusive access to students, teachers, parents, and school managers.

For further information, please visit www.dsop.com.br/escolas or contact a local franchisee in your area by searching on our website www.dsop.com.br/franquia.

What's happening

In the fourth volume of the series, Money Boy and his friends learn how to fight for a more sustainable world while they all learn to take care of a new friend that really needs their help.

Lagoa Branca, where Money Boy's adventures take place, is changing fast and getting new bus lanes and new companies that have settled in town. Meanwhile, its inhabitants learn how to use technology in their daily life. All that without keeping their attention on a very important subject nowadays: sustainability, being it environmental, social and financial. Money Boy and his friend learn new financial education lessons, find out what are the 5R's that are key-issues for a healthier life, and face the challenge of making a collective dream come true.

A new student arrives at school, sweet Caroline, who rapidly becomes friends with all of them. The plot also unveils a new character that will need their help more than anyone: Nino, the puppy.

© Editora DSOP, 2016
© Reinaldo Domingos, 2015

President
Reinaldo Domingos

Text editor
Andrei Sant'Anna
Renata de Sá

Art editor
Denise Patti Vitiello
Christine Baptista

Illustrator
Ariel Fajtlowicz

Editorial producer
Amanda Torres

English language version
Joan Rumph
Milena Cavichiolo

All rights reserved to Editora DSOP
Av. Paulista, 726 - Cj. 1210 - Bela Vista
ZIP Code: 01310-910 - Brazil - São Paulo - SP
Phone: 55 11 3177-7800
www.editoradsop.com.br

Dados Internacionais de Catalogação na Publicação (CIP)
(Câmara Brasileira do Livro, SP, Brasil)

Domingos, Reinaldo
   Money boy : in a sustainable world / Reinaldo Domingos ; illustration Ariel Fajtlowicz ; translation Joan Rumph e Milena Cavichiolo. -- São Paulo : Editora DSOP, 2015.

   Título original: O menino do dinheiro : num mundo sustentável
   ISBN 978-85-8276-117-5

   1. Dinheiro - Literatura infantojuvenil
2. Finanças - Literatura infantojuvenil
I. Fajtlowicz, Ariel. II. Título.

14-11969   CDD-028.5

Índices para catálogo sistemático:

1. Educação financeira : Literatura infantil
    028.5
2. Educação financeira : Literatura infantojuvenil
    028.5

Contents

No worries and big smiles 7

Back to school 11

The 5R's lesson 17

Computers, at last 23

Mr. Raymoney's new subject 27

Today's goodwill action 31

A sustainable friendship 35

Nino's club 39

A shared dream 45

What is DSOP? 51

Everything can become art 57

The big day 63

Celebrating at Daisy's Square 69

No worries and big smiles

During vacation, the town of Lagoa Branca seemed to slow down. The streets became empty without kids coming and going to school. Traffic was lighter and its residents seemed to enjoy the peaceful atmosphere.

Money Boy woke up in a happy mood. He could hear his sister Gaby crying in her crib, and his mother busy in the kitchen warming up her milk and cooking the family's breakfast. His father was moving around, getting ready for work.

With the arrival of the new baby, the family's routine had changed in many ways. Mrs. Foresight woke up earlier than she used to, and her sleeping hours had to adapt to her daughter Gabriela.

Mr. Unaware worried about the family´s expenses, since they increased. Now he was responsible for his wife, his son, and his little girl, who needed diapers, milk, clothes, a stroller, and many other things.

Mrs. Foresight could not leave home for work as she used to, because she kept busy with her baby. She didn't go out to visit her customers as often as before.

One thing was becoming clearer at Money Boy's home; expenses had gone up and the family's income had gone down.

However, vacation time was almost over and Money Boy knew that he'd soon go back to school, meet his friends, and continue his lessons.

Maybe talking to Mr. Raymoney, who had given him valuable advice about his life, would be of some help this time, too.

Victoria, on the other hand, had traveled to her grandparent's cottage and didn't realize classes were starting soon. Mrs. Efficiency had to call her and say she should come back home by Sunday, the last day of the month, to organize her school supplies and get ready for the new school year.

Spender was anxious to meet his two friends once again and tell them about his new computer. The boy spent his whole vacation learning how to use the Internet.

Not very far from there, Caroline, a girl with blonde hair and a mysterious look on her face, had recently moved to town. She observed, through the window of her room, the coming and going of people on the streets. Caroline spent time riding her bike on the streets nearby and getting to know the area.

She had moved to the same neighborhood where Money Boy, Victoria, and Spender lived.

They hadn't met her yet, but, coincidently, she would be going to the same school as them, and, soon, they would be seeing each other on a daily basis.

In the previous year, the three friends and their classmates had learned about the **DSOP Methodology** and, during the last semester, everybody was involved with entrepreneurial lessons taught by Mr. Raymoney.

The beginning of the school year promised to be thrilling, full of surprises, and classes even more challenging for the students. They certainly would live up to the name of their school called Growing Up Together.

For now, the children of Lagoa Branca didn't have a clue as to what was about to happen. They all wanted to enjoy the remaining vacation days with no worries and big smiles on their faces.

Back to school

On the first day of school, all the students followed the signs on the walls and looked for their new classrooms.

Money Boy, one of the first to arrive, greeted Mrs. Constance, who had been their art teacher for many years.

A few minutes later, several kids entered the door to the classroom talking very loud and making a racket. Everyone wanted to tell each other about their summer vacation and all the latest news.

The girls showed off their new hairdos, the boys displayed their new backpacks, and everyone anxiously recalled the adventures of those long months that had seemed unending. One thing not lacking in the classroom was a subject to talk about with their friends.

In the midst of the noise, Victoria captivated her friends with a new set of notebooks created by her mother's company. The girls wanted to know the price, the number of sheets, if there were other styles, and more.

Mrs. Constance walked over and examined one of the notebooks made from recycled materials. She admired the cover constructed with corrugated paper and decorated with colorful fabric glued on top.

A variety of beautiful fabrics made the notebooks even prettier. The inside sheets were recycled paper, sewed at the margins, and tied up with a wide satin ribbon.

The handcrafted work was exquisite. Victoria's mother had set up a business called Recreate, and the notebooks caused a boost in sales for the company.

Nevertheless, the teacher wanted to start the class and asked all the students to be silent and take their seats so that she could address all of them.

Since the students had showed interest in the notebooks, she began by welcoming everyone and asking them an intriguing question.

"I want to use these notebooks as an example and propose something that has to do with our research project for this year," said Mrs. Constance. "Can anybody tell me how many sheets of paper are wasted in a school per year?"

The class quieted down for a few seconds and then the teacher continued.

"Have you seen the amount of waste we have in our trash can at the end of the day?" she asked. "Let's imagine the following: We have ten classrooms at this school. If each one of them wastes three sheets of paper per day, we have thirty sheets wasted, and that refers to afternoon classes only. Let´s say we have 22 days of class in a month, how many sheets are thrown away?"

Money Boy raised his hand, as he was good at math and quickly answered.

"Six hundred sheets, teacher."

"Very good, Money Boy. How about per year?" Mrs. Constance asked, challenging the students.

The class remained silent.

"In one year, we waste up to six thousand sheets, not to mention those sheets we doodle onto and then throw out, and that old notebook that goes into the garbage without having all of the sheets used up. Little by little, our wastepaper turns out to be a mountain of paper," added Mrs. Constance.

"Teacher, my father told me several trees are cut down to make paper," Victoria commented.

"That's right Victoria! For every 110 pounds of paper produced, a tree is cut down. Therefore, it is important to know that when we recycle paper, we also avoid the destruction of nature. Think about how many trees could be saved if we reused the sheets in our notepads, notebooks, and diaries," said Mrs. Constance. "That's why this year we are developing a project about recycling."

"But what is recycling?" Spender asked, scratching his head.

"Recycling is reusing anything. For example, Victoria's mother used leftover fabric she normally would throw away, but instead, she made beautiful covers for the notebooks. In addition, she reused sheets of paper that probably would have been wasted. By reusing materials, she created something new, exquisite, and useful," Mrs. Constance explained.

"My father brings back home all the leftover paper from his work. Before, everything was thrown away, but now my mother is using it to make the notebooks. I have lots of fun helping her out and suggesting patterns and colors for the stamps and ribbons she uses," said Victoria without hiding her enthusiasm.

"That's a very good example, Victoria. Recycling is essential at schools, offices, and inside our own homes as well. We need to practice and encourage other people to do so. We'll soon talk a lot more about it," Mrs. Constance said.

The students started to think about the subject and then the teacher wrote on the board the theme of the classes for that semester: Conscious Consumption—The Lesson of the 5R's.

Mrs. Constance was thrilled with the success of her first class of the year by introducing the subject before the curious eyes of her students:

"This semester we'll be speaking about conscious consumption. Consuming in a conscious way is using things with moderation, without excess, and avoiding waste," Mrs. Constance began to explain. "Let's think about practical and smart ways to save the earth's natural and financial resources. We need to build a better place for us to live, become more sustainable, and preserve our world for children in the future."

"What about that 5R's rule you mentioned," Victoria asked.

"Well, that will have to wait until the next class. I want you to form groups and think about everything we've talked about today."

The students were anxious, hoping for the next class so they could learn more about the 5R's.

The teacher then ended the class by saying, "We have a long road ahead of us, and I can assure you that our lessons will turn you into better and more conscientious people."

The bell rang and the students rushed out of the class all at once. The school was alive, full of children and teenagers running up and down the halls.

The buzz about new things took over the place and Victoria, Money Boy, and Spender had something new to share.

The 5R's lesson

The following day in the school cafeteria, the three friends drank some juice and told stories about their last two months of vacation.

"Tell me, Money Boy, how's your little sis doing?" Victoria asked.

"Oh, she's still too small. She can't talk, play soccer, or stuff like that. She's only eating and sleeping. Ah, and sometimes it gets worse—she cries her heart out. Isn't it incredible that crying is the only thing newborn babies know how to do? And most of the times I don't even know why she cries, much less what to do to make her stop," Money Boy complained.

"Babies are just like that. There's no fun in the beginning. But let me tell you something!" said Spender, changing subject.

"Speak up! If we don't let you, you're going to tell us anyway," said Money Boy, laughing.

The three of them laughed.

"Guess what? I got a laptop computer as a gift. I've learned to surf the Internet and it's so cool," revealed Spender.

"Wow, that's cool," said Victoria. "Can we use it to do some research about recycling?"

"Of course. We can watch cool music videos, discover new bands, and play games online," Spender said.

"Can we play online with other people? My cousin told me there are some cool games online and there are even championships. Is that true?" Money Boy asked.

"Yes, we can do everything you're talking about and much more. I just don't know how to do everything yet," Spender answered with a grin.

"No problem. We can learn together then," said the girl with dimples.

Spender showed Money Boy and Victoria the research pages on his laptop.

"Look how light and practical it is. I can take it inside my backpack wherever I go."

"Ah, and there's even a more modern one. It's called a tablet," Victoria informed her friends. "It's the size of a book more or less. Having a tablet is a dream I have, now that we are going to have computer classes. Have you seen one of those?"

"Yes, they're cool but more expensive," Money Boy replied.

"That's true. My mother and I went to some stores to compare prices. You know, I'm saving part of my allowance to buy one of them at the end of the semester," Victoria said.

"Changing subjects, have you noticed the new student in our class?" asked Money Boy.

"I have and I found her a little weird," said Victoria. "Her honey-colored hair, the way she walks, I don't know.

Haven't you noticed anything?" Spender asked.

"She has a ponytail! The girl acts like a snob. In fact, she didn't open her mouth during the whole class. Really weird," Victoria said.

The conversation was not over, but the bell rang and the three friends had to go back to the classroom for another hour with Mrs. Constance.

The teacher started talking about the 5R's Lesson:

"Students, today we are going to learn what the 5R's are. They will ensure that we hold ourselves as conscious consumers, aware of the natural and financial resources we have at home, here at school, and everywhere we live on this planet. They are Reduce, Reuse, Recycle, Refuse, and Recreate."

Mrs. Constance suggested a shared reading of the first chapter of the book they had about conscious consumption.

"Spender, start reading what we have about the first R, please," said the teacher.

"The first R is Reduce. To Reduce is being aware of the amount we spend on anything and creating ways to cut down our excessive consumption," the boy read.

"Mary, would you please give us an example of that?" Mrs. Constance asked.

"I think a good example of that is the amount of time we spend taking a shower. A shower can last 10-15 minutes or maybe even half an hour. We get distracted by our thoughts and end up wasting water, which is a very important natural resource for us," the girl answered.

"Very good. By reducing water consumption and using it wisely, we are contributing to the sustainability of the planet," added Mrs. Constance.

"Mrs. Constance, can I read about the second R?" Victoria asked.

"Yes, dear. Please share it with us."

"Well, the second R stands for Reuse, which means using the same thing several times before throwing it in the garbage. Disposable plastic plates, for example, can be washed and used again for another meal," Victoria said.

"The third R means Recycle," advised Money Boy. "To Recycle is to find a new way to use an object still in reasonable condition, which typically would be thrown away."

"That's right, Money Boy. Could you please give us a practical example of recycling?" the teacher challenged him.

"Well, I just remembered something my mother usually does at home. She buys jelly that comes in a jar, and when we finish eating it, we use the jar as a drinking glass."

"That's great! A glass jar normally is thrown in the garbage after its content is gone. Nevertheless, Money Boy's mother applied the third R lesson and recycled it."

Phillip, who sat behind Money Boy, raised his hand and volunteered to read about the fourth R.

"The fourth R is Refuse, which is choosing products that do not harm the environment. For example, when my mother goes grocery shopping, she brings along cloth bags to carry her purchases and refuses to accept those plastic bags that pollute the environment."

"Well done, Phillip! That is a very good example of a sustainable habit," said Mrs. Constance. "And lastly, I'm going to ask Mariana to please tell us what the book says about the fifth R."

"Well, the fifth R is Recreate and has a lot to do with what Victoria's mother does at her company. Recreate means to invent ways of using stuff that would normally be discarded, and then produce other objects for our use or even for decorating purposes. Products made by the company, Recreate, are good examples of that. They make notebooks and diaries out of leftover fabric, string, and recycled paper," the girl said.

With the final presentation made by Mariana, Mrs. Constance said the class was over and the students went out for a break.

In the schoolyard, Money Boy spotted Mr. Raymoney coming out of the teacher's room and ran up to him. After their greetings, Money Boy revealed he was anxious to talk to him about a delicate matter.

"My dad is facing a dire situation at home," Money Boy started to explain. "With the arrival of a new baby in our family, our expenses have increased too much. To make things worse, my mother is no longer able to manage her door-to-door sales of cosmetics. Because of that, we have lost part of the money she made to help with our household expenses."

"I see. That often happens when a couple decides to have a baby," Mr. Raymoney reasoned. "Your parents are spending more and earning less. That is, the family's expenditures are larger than their income. However, there are some practical alternatives."

"Well, I can't see any alternatives and don't know what to do to help them, because kids can't work for a living. I look forward to the day when I am old enough to have a job and can help my father with expenses at home," Money Boy said.

"Take it easy. Everything in its own time," the teacher said. "You are already helping by focusing on your studies and being aware of the financial principles that you've learned at school. But, as for your parents' situation, I might have a couple suggestions."

"Then tell me now!" the anxious boy said.

"Hand this brochure to your father," said Mr. Raymoney. "It's about specializing and specialized professional training in several job areas. The city, through a partnership with the state government, is providing courses to help professionals expand their skills in their current job. Your father could become a technician in his branch of work and get a promotion or maybe a change in his job or area of interest. People, who take courses and increase their knowledge, often get higher salaries."

"Thank you, Mr. Raymoney. That sounds great. I'm sure my father will learn quickly, because he's very smart," Money Boy said, as he grabbed the brochure from the teacher's hands.

"I'm happy to help. As for your mother, many women work at home. She might be able to perform activities without having to go out every day. Sewing is one of them, for instance. Did you know there are people who earn good money just for typing pages and pages of documents without leaving home?" asked the teacher.

"There are plenty of jobs like that. It's up to your mother to think about what she enjoys doing, which she can accomplish in your own home. I suggest that you have a discussion about it in a family meeting, because that way everyone can share their ideas," Mr. Raymoney said.

With his hope renewed and an expression of relief on his face, Money Boy said good-bye to his teacher. He knew the advice was valuable, and he would profit from it by helping his parents improve their family's financial situation. He felt confident everything would work out fine and that it was just a matter of time.

Computers, at last

Friday finally arrived, the day the students met their new teacher, Mrs. Sunday. She came into the class, introduced herself, and wrote on the board Computer Class-Room 910.

"Today, we'll be starting a new and very important subject, which is computer skill," she said, smiling at the intrigued faces of her students.

"Let's move to the computers in room 910. Please stand up in an orderly way, no mess…" She didn't even finish her sentence, when everyone went running down the halls, heading toward the room where they had never been to before.

The students were anxious to be attending computer class at last. In previous years, only the older students had been allowed to put their hands on the keyboards. This new group of students now felt it was their turn to figure out how everything worked.

"Students, since we don't have enough computers for everybody, I'm splitting the class up into pairs. We will draw names so you can pair up with a partner whom you have not worked with before," Mrs. Sunday explained.

Some students were thrilled while others seemed annoyed, because they still wanted to pair up with their best friends.

The teacher called their names at random, but coincidentally, Victoria and Spender ended up together. As for Money Boy, he teamed up with Caroline—the mysterious, new student with the blonde ponytail.

During the first ten minutes, Mrs. Sunday taught basic instructions for operating a computer: turning it on, connecting, and turning it off.

Money Boy, a little awkward with his new classmate, tried to act nice and introduced himself.

"Hi, my name is Ray. What's yours?"

"I'm Caroline," the girl said.

"You can call me Money Boy. It's my nickname here at school."

"Ah, cool."

"How do you like the school?" the boy asked.

"Frankly, I can't answer that yet. I don't know anybody," the girl replied.

"But now you know me. I'm somebody!" Money Boy said with a funny smile.

"Great. That's true," whispered the girl, without giving Money Boy much importance.

On the other side of the room, Victoria and Spender easily typed away on the keyboard. The computer was like a new toy and both of them enjoyed learning how it worked.

Mrs. Sunday showed the students the interactive section on the DSOP Financial Education website. Over the next few classes, they'd get used to the games and online activities that would complete the lessons about the **DSOP Methodology**, which they had studied with Mr. Raymoney.

The class was hectic, but learning how to use the computer for their schoolwork fascinated the students. From now on, they could learn various school subjects by playing games, answering fun tests, and much more.

Some of them already had computers at home, while others did not, but one thing became certain. A new world existed inside that little screen, and all the students wanted to unveil the mysteries of each website, each piece of software, and each window they laid their eyes on.

Mr. Raymoney's new subject

After computer class, the happy students welcomed Mr. Raymoney one more time. Financial education classes were their favorite.

While everybody else took notes of the teacher's writings on the board, Victoria had her eyes on Money Boy. He was the only one not holding a pencil and taking notes. Instead, his eyes starred at the new girl with the ponytail. Caroline seemed to draw the attention of several other boys in the class, too, who had their eyes on her.

Victoria doodled in her notebook and wondered, What's so special about that stuck-up girl?

Everybody turned their attention to the teacher when they heard the word "sustainability."

"This year, we are going to learn a new step in the world of financial education—the sustainability of a business," Mr. Raymoney announced.

"I don't think I'm getting it," Spender let out.

"That's pretty normal, Spender. We're just beginning to talk about it. Let me explain better. The word sustainability reminds you of what other word?" the teacher asked.

"Sustain," Victoria answered.

"Very good. Sustain or support. That is, when we start up a business or an enterprise. What can we do so it can sustain and support itself? What should we do in order to keep it working and achieving good results? Most of all, how can we work together with others in this world we are living in?" Mr. Raymoney asked.

"For companies and factories to help the world, they must be sure not to harm the environment, for example," Caroline responded.

"Great answer! You're new around here, aren't you? What's your name?" asked Mr. Raymoney.

"My name is Caroline. I used to live in another town where people worked in a huge factory, which caused a lot of air pollution. Children became sick and employees were always coughing and going to hospital, until the city council closed down the factory," the girl explained.

"You've mentioned an important point about sustainability, which is the relationship between enterprises and environment. Every business owner must take into account the issue of nature conservation, for example, the air we breathe, the animals, and the health of all of us. That means environmental sustainability," the teacher said.

After Mr. Raymoney's explanation, he read to the classroom the three basic concepts of sustainability he had already written on the board.

1) Environmental Sustainability: everybody must take into account the issue of nature conservation, the environment, and ensure the well-being of the place where you live.

2) Financial Sustainability: everybody should worry about renewing their resources in order to earn money and, when it comes to big businesses, creating new items for sale is essential. This way, as we saw last semester, it will create new opportunities for businesses and will keep people interested in buying those products that an enterprise sells. The most important thing is to spend less than you earn.

3) Social Sustainability: everybody should try to contribute to the social well-being of their neighborhood in the town where they live. As for businesses, they could generate jobs in the area where those companies are located.

"Can anyone please give me a good example of financial sustainability?" Mr. Raymoney asked.

"Yes, Recreate, the company that my mother started last year by selling notebooks made only of recycled materials," Victoria said. "At the end of the year, she noticed that the sales were going down and then she began making diaries and agendas for the New Year. This way people started buying again from us to give the new items as Christmas presents."

"Victoria, nice example! Your mother's company complies with two items written on the board. The recycled materials help prevent cutting down trees and encourages the reuse of fabrics and papers. That's the environmental sustainability of Recreate. By making agendas and diaries, your mother has created a new sales opportunity and it ended up very well. New products sustain the public's interest in buying from the same company. Nevertheless, it's important to emphasize that the real financial sustainability of any business rests in its balance: never spending more money than what comes in. The secret is to have revenues larger than expenditures. Do you remember that?" the teacher asked.

Victoria thought for a moment, and Mr. Raymoney took that opportunity to ask her another question.

"What can you tell me about the third rule right there called Social Sustainability?" asked Mr. Raymoney, pointing to the board. "Is Recreate worried about that as well?"

"Well, that I don't know," Victoria replied a little embarrassed. "I think that we haven't given it much thought yet."

"From now on, together we'll use our class time to think about that and other important issues as well," the teacher said.

The bell rang and class ended. On his way out, Money Boy said good-bye to his friends and walked home. Victoria recalled what the teacher had said as she walked home. Mr. Raymoney's lesson had brought to her attention something she and her mother had never thought of—Recreate's social sustainability.

Today's goodwill action

As he turned the corner, Money Boy spotted Caroline. She stood on the other side of the street next to a sad-looking puppy with long floppy ears. The puppy looked scruffy and in need of a bath.

Out of sheer curiosity, Money Boy walked over and tried to engage in a conversation.

"Hi, Caroline! Is that your puppy?"

"Unfortunately not," she said, sounding upset.

"Then why are you here with it?" the boy asked.

"I found him lying in the street yesterday. He was crying and he has a broken leg. I picked him up and put him under that tree. Then I went to the drugstore, bought a bandage, and wrapped his leg," Caroline explained.

"Poor thing. Seems like a street dog," Money Boy observed. "A car must have hit him and, in that case, your bandage won't last long. He needs to see a vet."

"You're right, but I'm new in town. I don't know of any clinic and I can't take him home either, because my mother would never let me have it. She hates pets," Caroline sighed.

"Well, I can ask my mother to take him to the vet, and maybe she will agree to let him stay at home with us, at least until he gets better," the boy suggested.

"Really?" the girl's watery eyes looking up, hoping it was possible.

"Yes, let's pick him up without moving his little leg. My house is only two blocks away," he said, pointing toward his home.

"Wow, that's really nice of you. I wanted to help Nino out, but I just didn't know how," Caroline confessed, taking the puppy gently in her arms.

"Nino?" the boy asked.

"Yes, that's the name I gave him. Take a look, doesn't he look like Nino?" asked Caroline.

"Sure. Nino is a great name," the boy agreed.

When Mrs. Foresight saw them both coming through the door holding the injured puppy, she became so touched that she embraced their cause at once and took the dog to a vet nearby.

The vet examined and treated Nino, and gave him a good bath. The dog got the best possible treatment while Caroline and Money Boy remained in the waiting room.

After much talking, Money Boy and his new friend convinced Mrs. Foresight to let the dog stay in the yard while he was recovering. They stated that taking care of a homeless dog would be their goodwill action.

The boy told his mother all he had learned from Mr. Raymoney's lesson about social responsibility and common well-being. Mrs. Foresight felt proud of her son for being so aware and capable of that goodwill gesture and allowed Nino to stay in their house.

Caroline and Money Boy left the vet with their hearts filled with joy. The little dog still limped, but he would get better soon with the loving care of his new friends.

Within a short time, the girl and the boy would find out many important things about taking care of a pet. Playing with the puppy and petting him isn't enough. A pet demands a good deal of material things so he can survive, such as food, vaccines, a collar, medicine, a bed, toys, and all of that requires money.

A sustainable friendship

The following week, Money Boy arrived worried and breathless at school and looking for Caroline. Victoria and Spender found it strange that he and that new girl, who was so silent and mysterious, now had become friends.

The girl with the blonde ponytail sat in the cafeteria eating a grilled cheese sandwich when Money Boy came over.

"Caroline, my mother just told me we can't have Nino at home anymore. He is chewing on everything. He grabs the clothes from the hanger and tosses them on the ground. The worst is that my little baby sister is allergic to his fur. She keeps sneezing, so my parents told me enough is enough. Besides, my father talked very serious to me about spending money on dogfood, medicine, trimming, and other expenses that will show up along the way," Money Boy stated.

"We've got a problem then. Poor Nino. What can we do now?" the girl asked.

"I don't know. We have until the end of the day to figure something out," Money Boy said, going over to the register to buy a snack.

The boy's face looked tense. He ordered a burger and a glass of juice. Caroline appeared concerned for him.

"What? What are you looking at?" the boy asked sharply.

"Do you eat meat?" she asked.

"Sure. Don't you?" he said, a little scared of his response.

"Of course not!" Caroline blurted out. "Do you know they had to slaughter a cow to sell you that burger? An animal just like Nino, and he had a family of his own, dreams of his own, a whole life ahead of him."

The girl almost gave a speech, her ponytail swindling with each gesture she made.

The boy looked at her, then to the woman who was about to put the burger inside the bread, and backed up.

"Hold on, please! I'm changing my order. I want..." he said, looking at his friend's cheese sandwich. "The same thing she's having," he continued.

Caroline gave a big smile of approval.

They both ate their sandwiches without noticing Victoria and Spender had their eyes on them.

"Have you seen that?" asked the girl with dimples.

"I have. And I don't understand anything," answered Spender.

"She's a vegetarian," concluded Victoria.

"And what's that? Ah, I think I know. People that only eat vegetables, right?" Spender guessed.

"More or less," Victoria said. "Vegetarians don't eat any meat that comes from animals."

"But all meat comes from animals, right?" Spencer asked.

"Not all of them. There's soy meat, for example. I have a vegetarian cousin and she only eats soy meat," the girl informed her friend.

"Ah, that's interesting!" Spender mumbled in agreement.

"That's not interesting. Is Money Boy now doing exactly what that girl tells him to? He's not even hanging out with us anymore. He hangs around only with her," complained Victoria.

"Are you jealous?" Spender teased.

"Jealous? Me? No! If he doesn't want to be my friend anymore, he is the one who's missing out," Victoria said, sounding bitter.

"I see. Sometimes what we say is the opposite of what our heart wants," Spender hinted.

"Since when did you become a philosopher? Let's go back to the classroom. It will be much better than staying here," she told the boy, grabbing his arm.

In the classroom, Mr. Raymoney told the students to team up into small groups, and Money Boy invited Victoria and Spender to join him and Caroline.

Even though she felt a little annoyed, Victoria accepted the invitation so that nobody could say she was foolish enough to feel jealous.

The challenge now was to make up sustainability examples for a fictitious company. Using what they had learned in their computer classes, they would have to set up a blog to write about environmental, financial, and social sustainability.

After the first ten minutes of group work, Money Boy was feeling enthusiastic. Caroline and Victoria seemed to be getting along, at least on the subject of classwork and sustainability lessons.

The challenge from now on would be to develop that friendship into a sustainable one.

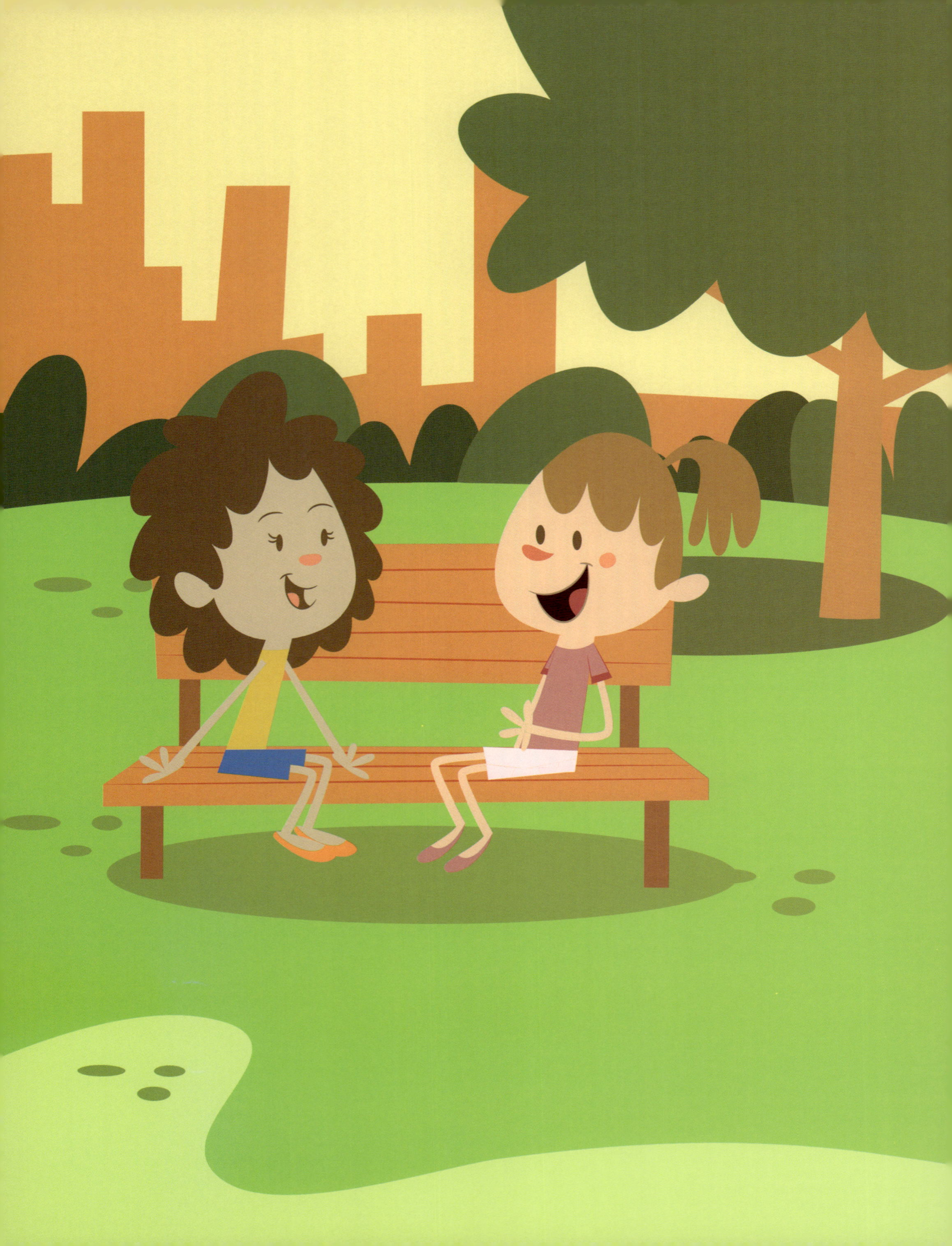

Nino's club

At the end of the day, Money Boy asked his friends to meet him at Daisy's Square, because he had an urgent matter to discuss and needed fresh, thinking minds to help him.

Caroline and Victoria were the first ones to arrive. They sat on a bench near a tree and did not speak until the girl with the ponytail decided it was about time to put an end to the silence.

"How many people live at your house?" she asked.

"My dad, my mom, and me," Victoria sad. "Why do you ask?"

"Nothing at all," Caroline replied, getting off the subject.

"And at yours?" Victoria asked.

"In my house there's me, my grandpa, and my mother," Caroline answered.

"Don't you have a father?" Victoria asked.

"I do. They are divorced. My dad lives in another town," said the girl with the ponytail.

"Ah, that's boring. It must be, I mean," Victoria said, feeling a bit awkward.

"Yes and I spend much time alone," admitted Caroline. "My mother travels a lot because of her job and my grandpa is often sleeping, but I'm used to it."

"Someday maybe you could come over and we can study together. I don't have any brothers or sisters, and I do my homework alone most of the time," said the girl with the dimples.

"Ah, thank you. Do you have a best friend?"

"No. How about you?" Victoria asked.

"Me neither."

They remained silent one more time. But the atmosphere in Daisy's Square became much lighter. Some minutes later, the two boys approached the girls.

Money Boy told Victoria and Spender all about Nino since the day he had helped him until last night, when his mother gave him a deadline to find the pet a new home.

They tried to find out a solution and eventually Victoria suggested an idea that could work out.

"Maybe we could set up the Nino's Club. Each day of the week one of us can host him at home. This way it is easier to convince our parents to have him over for one day and one night only, once every seven days. What do you think?" the girl asked.

"Victoria, that's an awesome suggestion!" Caroline shouted.

"Victoria is good at planning," Spender said.

"Cool, but then we need seven people to join this club of ours so that Nino can spend one day with each one," Money Boy maintained.

"You see, there's my cousin. He also studies here and loves pets. I think he will be up for it," said Victoria.

"I think Philip and Mary would also join us. Last year, their schoolwork in the arts class had to do with animal welfare," recalled Spender.

"Cool and there's the four of us, along with Philip, Mary, and Victoria's cousin. If they are all in, Nino will be safe and sound. Let's talk to them at once, because tomorrow my mother said she doesn't want to hear him barking in the house," said Money Boy, laughing.

After that, each of them hurried back home. Victoria went straight to her room with her head full of ideas.

She started to recall her earlier conversation with Caroline. Ever since Victoria had attended school, she had been hanging out with the boys mostly. She was friends with Money Boy, Spender, and Phil, and now she had met a girl.

The girl with dimples looked in the mirror and realized that having a girlfriend wouldn't be so bad. *It might be nice to have someone to advise me about my clothes, play with makeup, gossip about the boys...*

Suddenly, someone knocked on the door and interrupted her thoughts. It was her mother, Mrs. Efficiency. The girl took the opportunity to tell her all about the plan for Nino's club.

She needed to convince her to allow the puppy to stay with the family once a week. That was the secret mission for all the seven people associated with the club.

Mrs. Efficiency appreciated their plan and their organization to help dear Nino. However, she reasoned with her daughter that it could only be a temporary solution, until they found a permanent owner to keep the dog. She managed to convince the girl that it wouldn't be practical for the families nor for the little pet to change homes so often.

The girl's mother advised her to draw up a budget of all the necessary expenses for anyone who wished to have a pet at home. Afterwards, the club members could go out and look for someone who could afford to adopt the sweet Nino.

Victoria thought for a while and concluded her mother was right. The club members would have to meet at once to make the necessary arrangements for that to happen.

The girl with the dimples gave her mother a hug and thanked her for the wise advice. She was sure in the end everything would be fine and she and her friends, including her new best girlfriend, Caroline, would find the right person to adopt the beautiful little dog.

The next day, Victoria and Caroline took Nino to Spender's house. Convincing Mr. Custodio to let the dog sleep over every Tuesday was not that difficult.

The Nino's Club plan worked out and the puppy seemed happy, having so many kids taking care of him.

At school, Ms. Constance kept up her lessons about recycling and gave the class an assignment due by the end of the semester.

The students had to talk about their family and their daily routine through artwork made only from recycled materials.

"You can use soda caps, cans, plastic bottles, string, shoe boxes, or whatever would normally be discarded, and reuse these to create a work of art," the teacher instructed.

The students would receive a grade for their individual homework assignment, which would count as the final exam. Everyone enthusiastically tried to figure out how to talk about using things that could be recycled. It was a major challenge after all.

During the break, the four friends went for a snack at the cafeteria. Victoria and Spender had a hot dog while Money Boy and Caroline enjoyed a cheese sandwich.

It was becoming clearer that, although she wanted to be friends with the girl with the blonde ponytail, Victoria didn't like the fact that Money Boy had changed his eating habits because of her.

Later during Mr. Raymoney's class, the groups teamed up once again to move forward with the sustainability work. The other groups worked with fictitious companies, but Money Boy's group actually planned sustainable solutions for the company, Recreate, owned by Victoria's mother:

"I think we can start with financial sustainability," Victoria said. "The book says here that for achieving financial sustainability, the companies must keep their balance, revenues always larger then expenditures, and should also create new items for sale to attract consumer's interest and loyalty."

"I guess I have an idea about a new item that Recreate could produce to sell," Caroline told the group. "Besides notebooks, agendas, and blocks of notes, Mrs. Efficiency could make those girl's diaries, with small padlocks on the cover."

"That's a cool idea!" Victoria cried. "And I do happen to have one of those diaries at home with a padlock. I write in it almost every day. It's my long-time companion."

"I also keep a diary and sometimes I have to write in it to feel better when I'm sad and I record all my good moments, too," Caroline added.

Spender, who had his eyes stuck on the notebook screen, building Recreate's blog, didn't pay attention to what the girls were talking about and wanted to follow up on the conversation.

"Diaries? Are they notebooks?" he asked confused.

"Diaries are a type of notebook that girls use to write down their daily activities and the boys they are interested in," Money Boy summed up with a smile.

"Oh, I get it. But is it really necessary?" asked Spender, still not quite aware of what was going on.

"Ah, it's a girl's thing," replied Money Boy.

Victoria and Caroline weren't even listening to what the boys were saying. The girls kept busy talking to each other about the diaries and discussing possible patterns and colors. They decided to start the trend at school and the blog would be a place to window-shop, so everyone could choose their own model, size, and color.

At the end of the class, Victoria and Caroline went together to the bathroom and the two boys finished taking notes for the group.

"Why do they always go together to the bathroom?" Spender asked.

"Ah, it's a girl's thing. Don't start thinking too much about it or you'll go crazy. They sometimes do things no one can explain," Money Boy said.

"Yeah, right. Like writing diaries and talking about things we don't have a clue about," Spender agreed.

"Exactly!" Money Boy said, laughing loudly.

The girls came back from the bathroom and seemed happy with the way the group project was going. However, they still had to address Recreate's environmental and social sustainability:

"Well, our company is already into conservation as long as it uses recycled materials as basic stock, right?" Spender questioned.

"Yes, but maybe there's something that we can add to that," Victoria suggested.

"I agree," said Caroline. "Let's think it over for the next few days and we'll meet again to discuss it."

"How about social sustainability?" asked Money Boy.

The school bell rang, signaling the end of class. The four friends agreed to talk about that subject during their next group work.

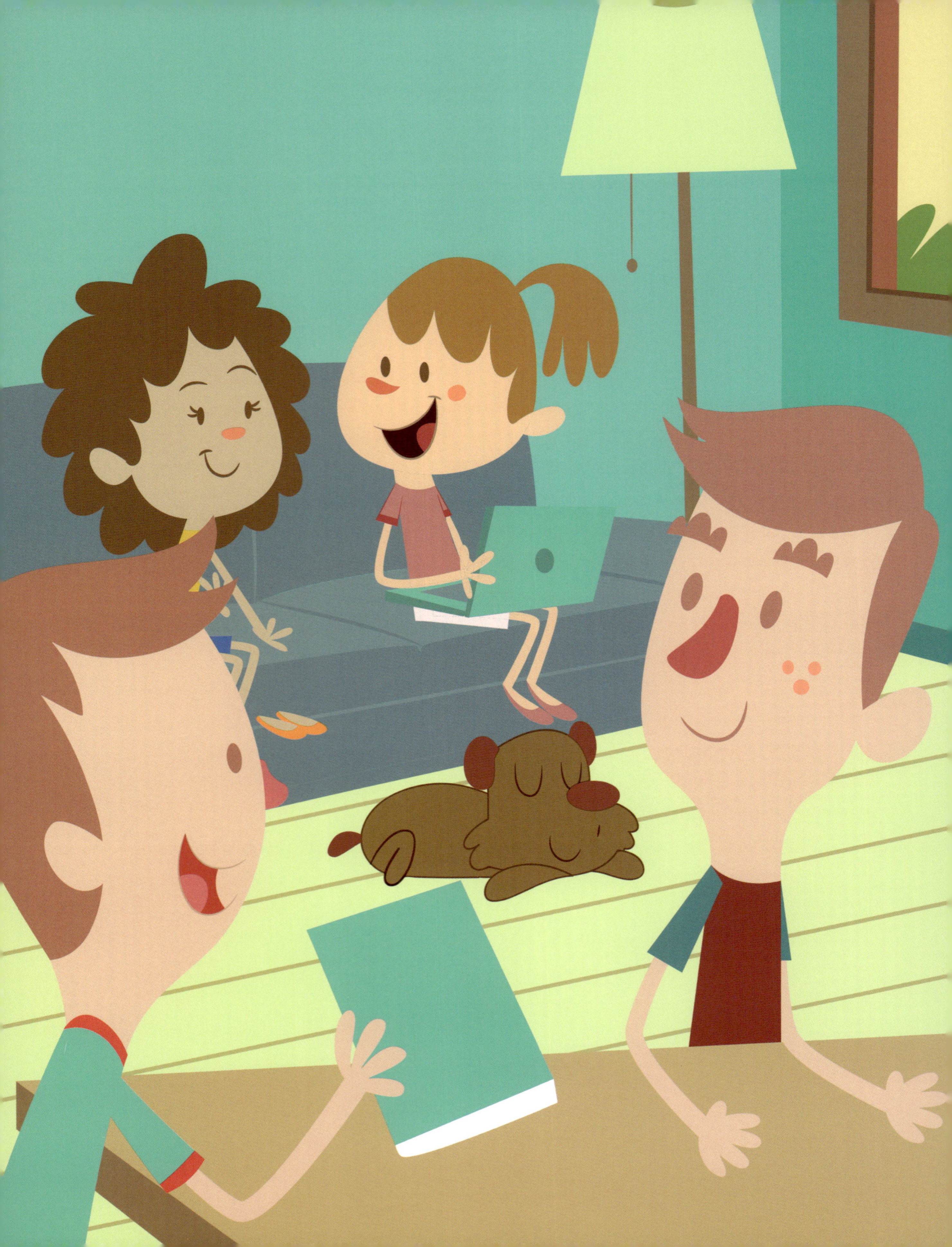

A shared dream

Several days went by and Nino's Club rotation scheme seemed to be working fine. Even Money Boy's mother had agreed to have the dog once a week at home, as long as he was kept in the yard, far away from little Gaby's allergic nose.

Besides that good news, Recreate's blog had gone online. Victoria's mother had already made some diary covers and Spender took their pictures and published them on the blog.

Students started to order them by e-mail. Money Boy became the webmaster and sent all the orders to Mrs. Efficiency. Meanwhile, Caroline and Victoria thought a lot about adding a social responsibility feature for the company to put into practice.

Conservation practices were already adopted by recycling things and reusing mountains of otherwise discarded paper that now would turn into notebooks, agendas, diaries, blocks of notes, and much more.

For the Recreate business to comply with the three rules of a sustainable company, it needed to engage in a productive relationship with the neighborhood within the town. However, the girls had not yet come up with an idea for doing that.

One afternoon, the four friends were together at Spender's house doing their homework. Nino followed everything closely and didn't take his eyes off of them.

The two girls saw Spender's computer on the table and decided to search the Internet on sustainability.

"Victoria, I've checked at the Town Hall website and saw they're looking for small businesses to adopt squares that need conservation. Do you think your mother could donate some money to help with our Daisy's Square, for example?" Caroline asked.

"Well, I can talk to her about that. The company is still very new. We don't have extra money to support a conservation project and that must be expensive," said the girl with the dimples.

Both kept searching and saw that generating jobs for people who lived in the neighborhood could be considered a social sustainability feature. Unfortunately, Victoria's mother had only two employees to help her. It was too small of a number to declare as an example of social responsibility.

Victoria came home thinking about what more they could do. She had to find out a solution to complete the sustainability project for her mother's company.

She entered her room and stood in front of the mirror. It had been quite a while, since she didn't talk to her faithful friend anymore.

She realized that maybe she didn't have to spend that much time speaking alone in the room, because now she had a best friend with whom she could share things.

During dinner, the girl tried to convince her mother to adopt Daisy's Square, but she knew that was not going to be an easy task.

"Dear, I realize the Recreate Company should cooperate with the conservation projects in our town. Unfortunately, we don't have the budget for that now," Mrs. Efficiency explained.

"What is a budget, mom?" the curious girl asked.

"Budget is the money that we separate to use on something more specific that we want to do," she said.

"I get it. What if you saved a small amount of money every month? That way you could help provide new benches and a playground for the square," the girl persisted.

"I don't think that's going to happen. Recreate is a small business and it is still crawling, dear," the mother replied.

Mr. Carrera, the girl's father, began to speak. "Honey, I do appreciate your worrying, but this is not the right time to insist on that. Why don't you talk to your friend, the one that is the heir of Custodio family's Cool Stuff ice cream factory? They could surely afford helping not only Daisy's Square, but many other green areas in town."

"Dad, you just gave me a great idea! If Cool Stuff adopted the Square alongside with mom's company, they could split the amount needed and everyone would be able to help. I'll talk to Spender and see if they can be responsible for the largest part. What do you say, mom?" the girl asked.

"Well, in that case things are slightly different. Go see them and find out what could possibly be done. I'm always willing to cooperate. It's just a matter of how," Mrs. Efficiency said.

Victoria went to bed a little more relaxed. She hadn't reached a solution yet, but something told her she was on the right path. What appeared to be a one man's dream was turning into a shared dream.

While she slept, someone else slept under her bed. The lovely Nino had come over from Spender's house and had quickly run straight to her room.

Back at school, Spender promised Victoria that he would talk to his dad about a joint social sustainability project and would get an answer as soon as possible. If Cool Stuff and Recreate developed a joint venture to take care of Daisy's Square, the students felt their work would be done.

Furthermore, Caroline approached the two of them and said she thought she had figured out a way for Victoria's mother to help the community using her own talent. Everybody was curious to know more about it and turned their eyes to her, waiting for her to give the details.

"Mrs. Efficiency could host a recycling workshop in poor neighborhoods of the town, let's say once a month during the weekends. This way other woman could learn the job and come up with things they could sell," explained the blonde-haired girl.

"Recycling workshop?" asked Spender.

"Sure! City Hall arranges lots of workshops like that with professional volunteers that go to a number of low-income communities and teach activities that can turn into a source of income to those families," added the girl with the swindling ponytail.

"Where did you learn all that, Caroline?" Money Boy wanted to know.

"The Internet. I read some articles and came up with the idea that Victoria's mother could use and so can we in our sustainability project," she answered.

"That's a great idea! I'll talk with my mom and see if she agrees, but I think it's okay," Victoria said.

"Anyhow, I'll talk with my father about the proposed revitalization project for Daisy's Square," said Spender.

"Do that. We have to cover all of our bases," agreed Caroline.

"By the way, whose turn is it to take Nino home today?" Money Boy asked.

"It's Philip's. He told me he would come over at the end of the day to take our mascot," Victoria answered.

Since the four friends wouldn't have their first class because Mrs. Constance had become ill, they decided to meet up under a tree in the schoolyard.

Victoria laid out a checkered tablecloth on the ground and all of them gathered for an important conversation with two agendas. They needed to discuss Nino's fate in the long run, and they had to outline the budget for the Daisy's Square conservation project.

Caroline showed her notebook with the figures she had come up with after some research with Victoria.

They checked the numbers that could be reduced slightly, but they came to a harsh conclusion. It would be difficult to find someone who could afford everything on the list.

Victoria and Caroline exchanged glances just as if they already had someone in mind to solve that problem.

They ran off to room 910 and asked to talk to Mrs. Sunday. The teacher allowed the girls in; she couldn't help but feel emotional about Nino's drama.

She had a 10-year-old daughter who dreamed of having her own dog. The teacher had even mentioned it to her students once. The story about Nino's hard times had touched her heart.

Victoria and Caroline showed Mrs. Sunday the list of dog expenses. She thought that perhaps she could afford the items. Still, Mrs. Sunday asked the girls for time to think it over. Victoria and Caroline were thrilled, but they would have to wait a little longer.

Costs for Raising a Pet

Monthly expenses:

Food: $20.00

Flea killing medicine: $10.00

Trimming and grooming (2x monthly): $20.00

Yearly expenses:

Collar: $10.00

Cushion bed: $15.00

Water and food bowls: $10.00

Vaccines: $80.00

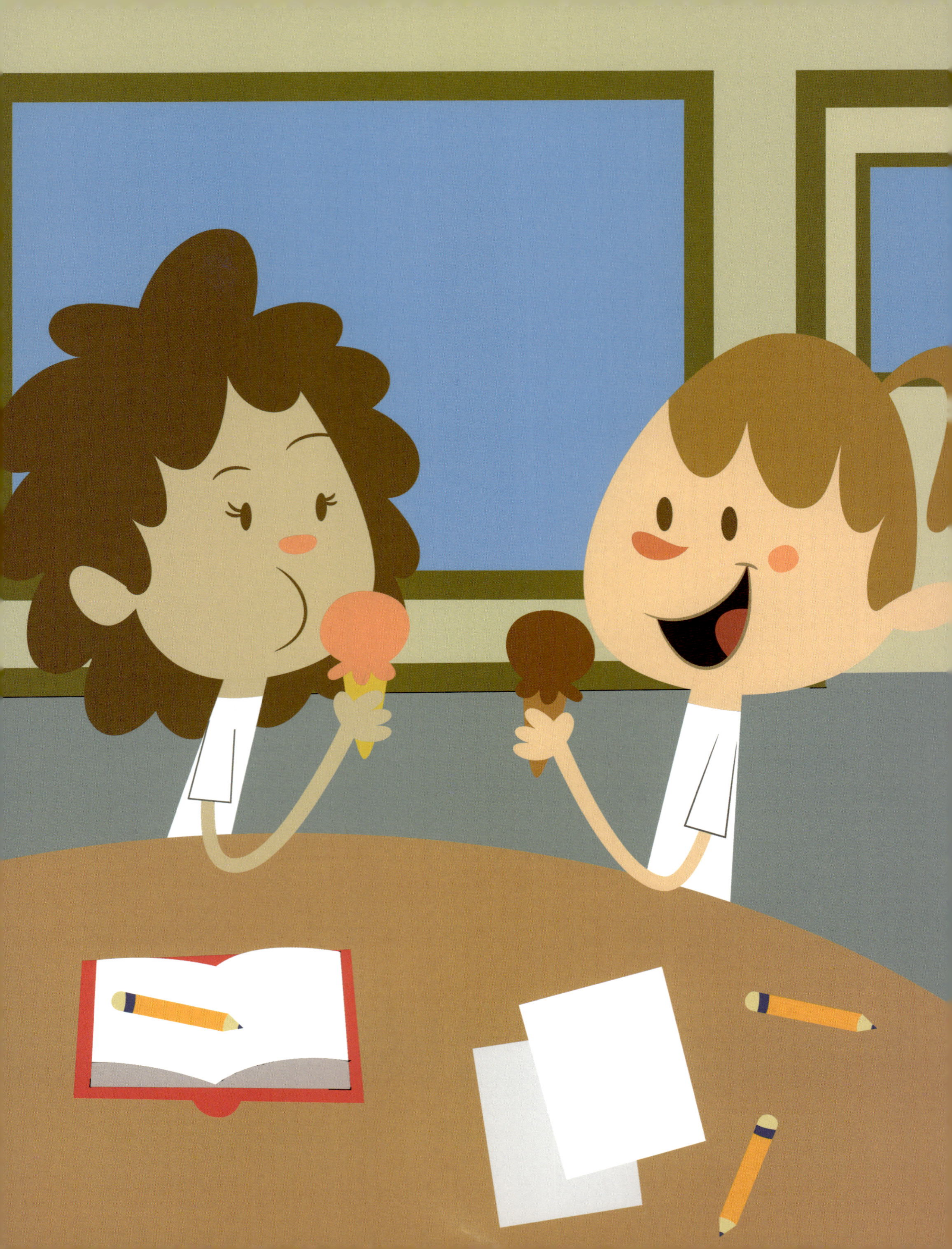

What is DSOP?

After talking to Mrs. Sunday, Victoria and Caroline noticed a friendship bond had grown between them.

Both had gotten together to make Nino's care budget. It was a hard work. They had to compare prices in pet shops and talk to a local vet as well.

Their struggle to get information and their desire to create a better future for the puppy had made Victoria and Caroline trust each other.

They decided to go for ice cream to celebrate their joint effort and their new friendship. They talked about many things and soon they were talking about their dreams. Victoria told Caroline she wished to purchase a computer by the end of the year.

Caroline listened carefully and became curious as to how her friend would make her dream come true. Then Victoria said she followed the four steps of the **DSOP Methodology**, and it helped her to pursue her dreams while her money remained in a safe place.

"What is DSOP?" Caroline asked.

Both of them laughed, and Caroline added, "I remember having heard that name before in the computer class. We had some games and activities borrowed from DSOP's website. I think it was something you were studying last year and, unfortunately, I hadn't move to town yet. In my other school, we didn't have financial education classes."

"Last year Money Boy taught me how to practice the **DSOP Methodology**," Victoria said. "I didn't know what it was either. Later on, Mr. Raymoney explained it to the whole class."

"Well, then if you could tell me what it is, I'd love to learn about it," Caroline said.

"Look, these four letters D-S-O-P mean Diagnosing, Dreaming, Budgeting, and Saving. It's an acronym that comes from the Portuguese language in which the method was written," Victoria explained.

"One of these words I know very well, dreaming," Caroline said, smiling.

"Dreaming is a wonderful thing. I think we are born knowing how to do it," added Victoria.

"But tell me, what is diagnosing? It's a medical term, right?" Caroline asked.

"Yes. When we are sick, the doctor tells us we need to have some tests in order to diagnose our condition," Victoria answered.

'That's true!" agreed Caroline.

"But that word can be used in other context as well. For example, you can make a diagnosis of your money and find out the financial health of your allowance," Victoria told her newest friend.

"And how can I diagnose my money today?" the girl asked.

"Every day you must write down your expenses in an expense notebook. Mr. Raymoney has several of them and we can get one for you," Victoria replied.

"When you record your expenses in a notebook, there is room for you to state the kind of expense and the amount you have actually spent. You must do that exercise for thirty days. Afterwards, you will have the diagnosis of your financial health and discover where your money is going. Only by completing this first step can you take the next one, which is Dreaming," revealed the girl with the dimples.

"Why must we diagnose our expenses?" asked Caroline.

"Well, that's important because, by the end of the thirty days, you'll be able to analyze your notebook and see if you're wasting too much money on things like bubble gum. We are hooked on bubble gum and that costs us money," Victoria admitted. "When I did my diagnosis last year, I found out I was using 10% of my allowance on buying gum every week. I was short of money before the end of the month and I didn't know why. After the diagnosis, I could spot many things that used up my money, useless things that drained my financial resources before my next allowance arrived," Victoria explained.

Caroline paid close attention and asked her friend to continue. Everything seemed to make sense.

"That's it! After the diagnosis, you'll be able to choose what to buy and what not to buy, according to your conscience. You will become aware that some things are useless and can be eliminated," Victoria said.

"Don't you chew bubble gum anymore?" Caroline asked.

"From time to time I do, but it's not a part of my routine anymore. It's not a habit I have to maintain. It has become something I do occasionally, and I'm not addicted to it any longer. The money I save will help me buy my tablet, which is something far more important to me. After all, this is my current dream," Victoria said with confidence.

"I understand you. What's more important, chewing gum or making a dream come true?" summed up Caroline.

"Way to go, girl! You've got the spirit," Victoria said.

"That's nice, that's really nice. I'm enjoying this chat. Tell me more about DSOP," Caroline urged her friend.

"Well the second step of the methodology is Dreaming. You have to choose three dreams to achieve. The first one is the short-term dream, one you would like to come true within six months. The second one is the medium-term dream, which can come true in about one year. The last one is the long-term dream and, to be achieved, it will take more than one year from now," instructed Victoria.

"That's very cool! I want to practice the **DSOP Methodology** and my short-term dream is going to be the same as yours, a laptop computer," revealed Caroline.

"Cool! We can dream together!" Victoria shouted.

"Yes, it's going to be awesome to share that joy with you!" Caroline cheered.

"Let's move to the third step then?" asked Victoria.

"Sure! I know what Budgeting is, but I don't have a clue of what it really means," answered Caroline.

"Most of our friends use their whole allowance within a month and don't save a single penny. In the **DSOP Methodology**, making a budget is taking part of the money you get every month and saving it in a piggy bank or in a savings account. Only after doing that can you use the rest of the money for your daily expenses," explained Victoria.

"Most people first spend and, if there's something left, they'll save a little. In DSOP Budgeting, you first save for your dream and then use the rest to cover the ordinary monthly expenses," Victoria said.

"Then I've got to know how much my dream is worth, the laptop computer, so I can have an estimate of how much I should save each month, right?" questioned Caroline. "Because I'm in a hurry and I want to have it as soon as possible!"

"You're smart, Caroline! You should compare prices at the stores and on the Internet. Look for different models, brands and prices to know exactly what you're getting, and how much it will cost," she advised.

"Yes. I'll do that, but how about the fourth step?" Caroline asked.

"The fourth step is saving. Saving means keeping your money in a safe place. The more money you are able to save, the quicker you can make your dreams come true," summed up Victoria.

"Hmmm… Where do you keep the money you save?" Caroline asked.

"I used to keep it in a piggy bank but nowadays I have a savings account that my mother helped me set up. Every time I deposit some money in the bank, the account gets a little bigger. And you know what's the coolest thing?" asked Victoria.

"What?" the girl with the blonde ponytail asked.

"There's something called the interest. Every time I put some money into my savings account, the bank adds to it a small amount of money, too. That's what we call the interest," said Victoria.

"What a fantastic thing. That's magical!" said Caroline with her eyes wide open.

"Yes! After I started practicing the **DSOP Methodology**, which is like a simple, magical formula, my dreams started to come true," Victoria said.

"I'm impressed!" Caroline said.

"Do you know why little Ray is known by his nickname Money Boy?" Victoria asked.

"No. No one has ever told me. Why is that?" she inquired.

"He was the first student to master the **DSOP Methodology**. Mr. Raymoney taught him the steps and he started practicing them. Next, Money Boy taught his parents the lessons and it changed the life of his whole family. When his piggy banks filled up with coins, he used that money to open a savings account. The bank always helps by adding a little extra money called interest, so he must have built a good financial reserve by now. That's why he is the Money Boy." Victoria explained.

"What an amazing story! My mother won't believe me when I tell her that!" Caroline remarked.

"We should teach it to everyone," Victoria announced.

"Yes, the **DSOP Methodology** sure is amazing!" Caroline nodded in agreement.

The two of them kept on talking and didn't even notice the sky had turned dark and they needed to go home. The **DSOP Methodology** was a thrilling subject, a magical formula that would open people's eyes to new possibilities.

Victoria went home feeling pleased that she had passed on the financial teachings to her friend, while Caroline felt enthusiastic for having discovered a smart way to make her dreams come true.

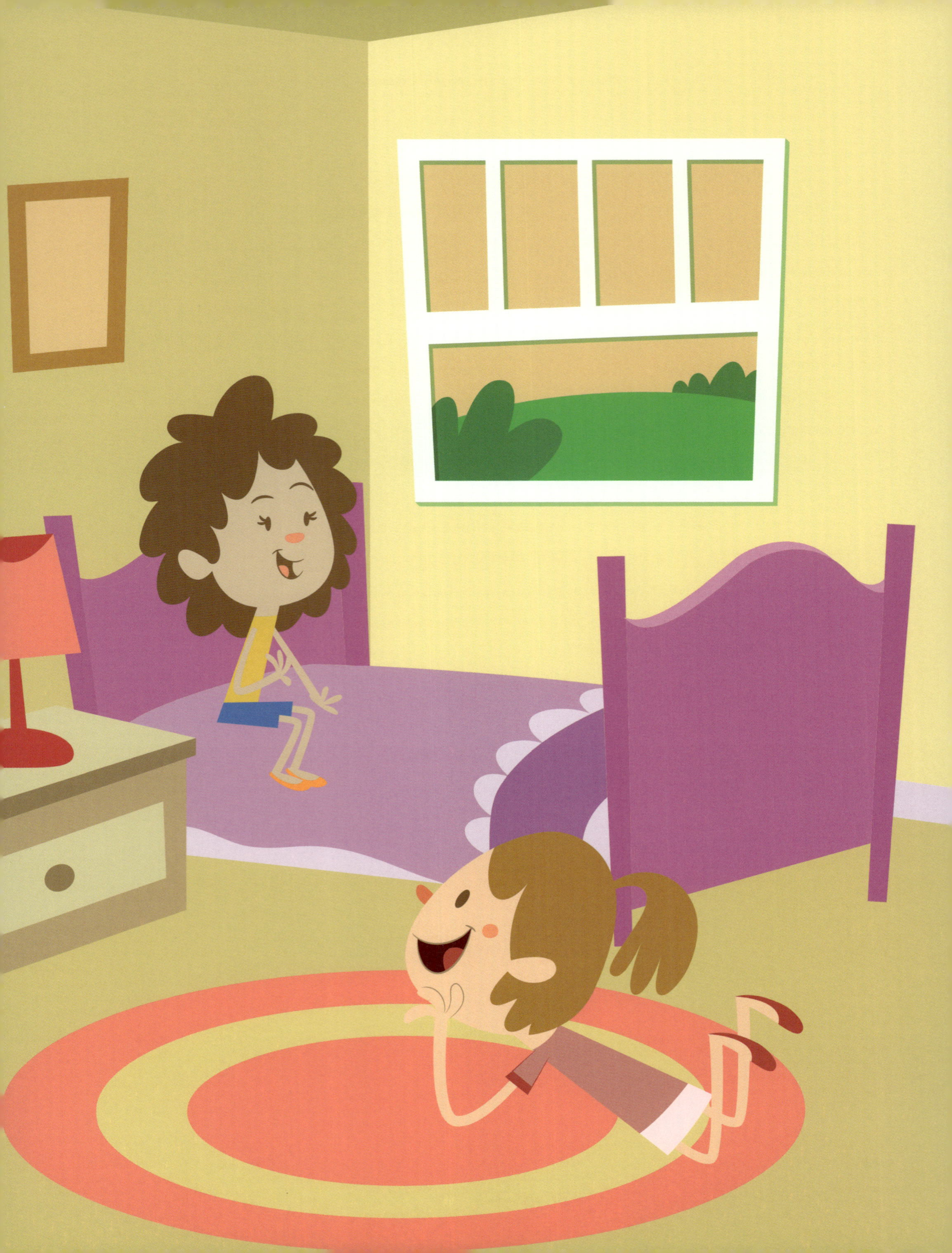

Everything can become art

Several weeks passed by and Lagoa Branca started to become full of activity, as new bus routes opened to connect the two sides of town.

A new international pizza restaurant opened downtown that increased the value to the area. The restaurant delivered all kinds of pizza to people's homes.

Other pizza restaurants used to do the same, except they took more than 35 minutes to deliver the pizzas.

Progress seemed to have finally arrived at the peaceful town of Lagoa Branca. Kids at the Growing Together School were learning new things every day.

One afternoon, Victoria invited Caroline over to her house. The two of them talked in Victoria's bedroom.

They chatted about several topics, such as boys, homework, the fate of Nino, improvements to Daisy's Square, and the **DSOP Methodology**, which both of them continued to stay engaged in.

These were thrilling subjects and the girls seemed happy. Victoria had found a friend with whom she could share her thoughts, and Caroline finally made friends in the new town.

The next day, both of the girls went to school feeling confident about their future. One girl showed strength and the other girl displayed joy—two very important traits for friends and partners.

It was good for both of them to know they could rely on one another whenever they needed to.

Finally, the day came to present their artwork. Ms. Constance asked all the students to show their work in front of the class and explain what it meant.

Spender explained his first. He placed a sailboat on the teacher's desk, which he had built by himself using discarded ice cream sticks. He had asked the man at the ice cream shop to collect the sticks for him so he could finish the work.

"This boat was made with recycled materials. I've managed to collect several wooden sticks that we usually throw away and glued them together until I finally built this sailboat. It represents my favorite pastime and my father's, too. We usually sail during the weekends and we have lots of fun," the boy said, grinning.

The rest of the class gave him a cheerful applause. Other kids presented their work until it was Victoria's turn.

The girl stood up and came closer to the teacher's desk. Facing her classmates, she explained, "Well, as my mother gathered many remnants of fabric at home, I got a few of the more colorful ones and sewed them together to make this beautiful tablecloth. Remnants are leftover pieces of fabric and cloth of all different textures and patterns. Tomorrow, I'll give the tablecloth as a birthday present to my Auntie Claire."

One after the other, the students showed their work, all of them very interesting. Then Mrs. Constance called on Caroline to present her work.

"My artwork is a book I wrote myself. I borrowed a few sheets of recycled paper from the company Victoria's father works for, and I filled up each page letter by letter and word by word. Then I made some drawings and created this cover in which the characters are all smiling and there is a little puppy beside them," described the girl with the ponytail.

The teacher asked her to hold the book up to display the drawings on the cover and inside the book, which helped tell the story.

Mrs. Constance thought the girl was a talented illustrator but she didn't make any remarks. She waited for Caroline to say why she created her work so different from the rest of the class.

"And what is your book about, dear?" the teacher asked.

"It's about seven friends who go to school together and decide to shelter a street dog named Nino. Their parents don't like the idea of having a dog in their home, so the friends come up with an ingenious plan to shelter the dog, to feed it, and to give it a home. If you want to know more, you'll have to read my book. I bet everyone will love it," said the girl cheerfully.

Mrs. Constance praised her for the work and for her creativity.

Finally, the teacher called on the last student, Money Boy, to show his creation. The boy stood up, walked to the center of the class.

"Well, I used empty tin cans as raw material. My mother helped me a lot and I couldn't have done this work without her. We made three piggy banks from the cans. Then we borrowed some paint from our neighbor and painted the piggy's to make them look more attractive for saving coins."

The class was rather surprised by the boy's idea. After all, everybody there had already learned of the **DSOP Methodology** and knew we must always have three dreams in mind.

Last semester's lessons from Mr. Raymoney were still alive in the minds of everyone. By seeing the three cans in different sizes, the students immediately identified the **DSOP Methodology** as an inspiration for Money Boy's work. The boy finished his presentation with the following remark:

"When I finished, I noticed these cans could also make good pencil holders as well. I took another used can and glued magazine pictures around it. It was so cool that I decided to give it to the teacher as a gift."

"Wow, Money Boy, what a beautiful gift. I'm going to put it on my study table next to my computer at home. I'll always cherish it. This is the result of a good lesson and work well done," said the teacher.

Before Mrs. Constance ended the class, she asked everyone to give all the students a round of applause and reminded them that they were coming to the end of the semester.

She wanted the students to do well in their other subjects, just as they had done in art. For some of them, that would pose quite a challenge.

While the students dealt with their lessons, Money Boy's mother still worried about the family's expenses at home.

She wanted to help her husband but didn't know how, because little Gaby still kept her from leaving home to sell her cosmetics.

When Money Boy came home and told Mrs. Foresight all he had seen and learned about in his art lesson, the two of them started to figure out a way to increase their family income.

The boy thought art could improve his home financial health or maybe just help in a small way.

As Money Boy watched his mother in the kitchen preparing to bake an orange cake, he had an idea.

"Mom, have you ever thought about cooking for other people?" he asked.

"No, son, I never have," she answered.

"Well, you're a fantastic cook, especially when you make desserts. Your orange cake is awesome, and I know you can make several other great desserts, like the ones people have at birthday parties. You know, mom, cooking is an art. Not everybody can do it the way you can," the boy praised her.

"Speaking like that makes it sounds easy. Cooking is something I love to do, and I could do it at home, even with your little sister always around. However, who would buy my desserts? People would not come down here just to buy a cake. I'd have to open a pastry shop and it would be very expensive," Mrs. Foresight told her son.

"But mom, nowadays with the Internet, many people sell things without actually having a physical store," Money Boy explained.

"What do you mean?" she asked.

"Well, we could set up a website to offer desserts and party food for birthday parties. We can add your telephone number and customers will call you to order what they want. For example, a child's birthday party for, let's say, 25 people. You can suggest the size of cake or the amount of desserts and food. Next, we can make everything for your customer and set up a delivery service," the boy continued.

"Son, what a wonderful idea! But are you sure people are willing to place orders with me? How will they know that now I am selling food?" asked Mrs. Foresight, still thrilled with the idea.

"Selling food? No way! You are a caterer. It's cooler to say it like that," emphasized Money Boy.

"That's true," the mother agreed.

"We could make some fliers and distribute them in town. In addition, I can create some buzz on the Internet and ask my friends to help me. There are many kids at school who host birthday parties throughout the year," the boy informed his mother.

"It's a marvelous idea for sure! Let's hear what your father thinks about it when he comes home from work. If he thinks it's a good idea, we can give that website and those fliers some serious thought," Mrs. Foresight said.

After the talking, Money Boy went to his room and Mrs. Foresight remained in the kitchen thinking about the idea. For the first time ever, she thought cooking might actually be a form of art. It certainly is a skill and not everyone is good at it.

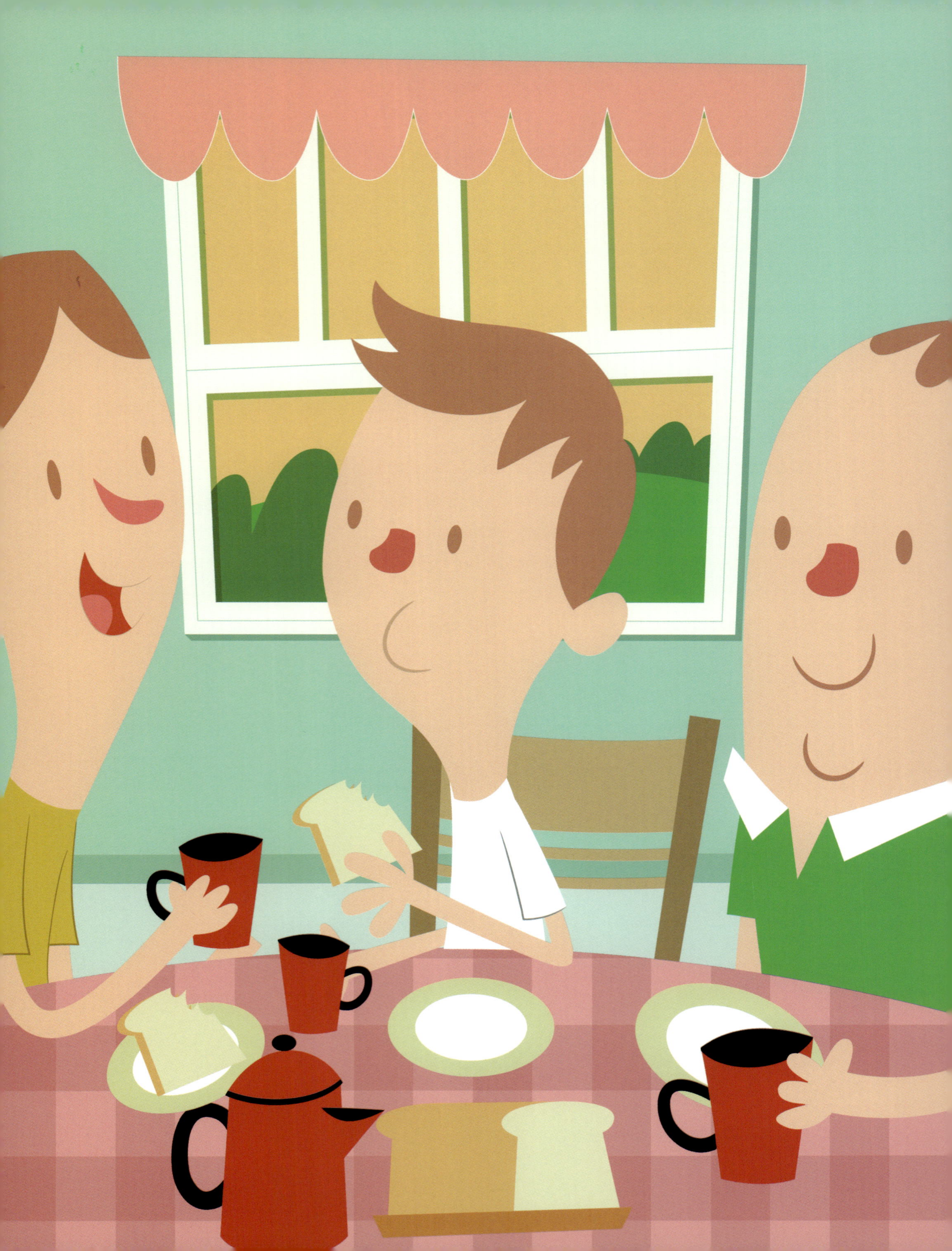

The big day

Time flew by in the town of Lagoa Branca. The end of the semester was near, and, with it, the day that students at the Growing Together School would present their sustainability work to Mr. Raymoney.

Money Boy appeared happy during the breakfast. His parents looked happy too, and his little sister Gaby wasn't crying as often. The family lived in harmony after Mr. Unaware agreed to the idea of his wife becoming a caterer.

At Victoria's house, Mrs. Efficiency woke up her daughter to tell her the good news. She had made a set of special diaries with tiny locks, so their future owners' secret information could remain private.

That sure was about to become a new sales hit both on the Internet and at the stationery shop. Victoria jumped off the bed to celebrate and asked to take one of the diaries to show the students in Mr. Raymoney's class.

As for Caroline, she had been up since early morning and ready to go to school. She showed her mother the book she had made for art class. Mrs. Smith took the book and flipped through the pages. She curiously asked her daughter, "Did you do it all by yourself?"

"Yes, mom," said the girl with a mischievous look on her face.

"The story about this puppy resembles Nino's own story, am I right?" Mrs. Smith asked.

"Yes, slightly. Only in my book the other Nino meets a female dog in the neighborhood and they have a date in the end," added Caroline.

"That's beautiful, honey. You've written a romance," Mrs. Smith remarked.

"Ah, is it called that? So be it. I've written a romance," the girl said, smiling.

"As far as I know, you've always said you wanted to be a vet when you grew up. What about now? Will you change your mind and think about becoming a great writer?" her mother asked.

The girl didn't answer and left home thinking about it as she walked to school. She met Money Boy, Spender, and Victoria all anxiously waiting for the bell to announce the start of Mr. Raymoney's class.

Some groups had already presented their projects. When they heard the name Recreate, the four friends stood up and approached the front of the room where a screen and a projector were set up.

They opened Recreate's blog and showed the class what the company did and how it had grown in the past year.

"The first concept we learned in Mr. Raymoney's class was about environmental sustainability. Since the beginning, Mrs. Efficiency, Recreate's production coordinator, has been concerned about using recycled material such as discarded paper, cardboard, and colored fabrics," Caroline began.

"Recreate is a home-based company, which doesn't harm the environment, doesn't litter, or annoy the inhabitants of our town," added Victoria.

"In order to meet the second sustainability concept, Mrs. Efficiency and her co-workers are always creating new products. The first ones were the colorful notebooks, followed by the agendas and notepads, and now the brand-new girly diaries. Besides, to keep its financial sustainability, the company is always concerned about spending less than its revenues, assuring its financial balance," explained Spender.

"These diaries feature small locks and keys. Only its owners will be able to open and read them," said Victoria, holding a pink and a light blue diary in each hand.

All the other girls in the class were delighted at seeing them. The teacher asked them to remain still so the group could finish their presentation. Money Boy took the opportunity to announce that the diaries are available to purchase on the company's website.

"I should add that the Internet has made it much easier for Mrs. Efficiency to advertise her products and control the customer's orders. Now that the blog is ready, we will hand over to her the passwords, so she or any of her co-workers can take care of everything from now on."

The teacher, impressed with the team's good work, asked them about the third concept called social sustainability.

"Recreate helps in any way possible to improve the neighborhood's social well-being. Now, with this Internet thing, my mother is considering hiring another employee to take care of the sales, because she and her two co-workers are always sewing things and don't have much time to be in front of the computer. By doing that, she is generating job openings for people in the neighborhood," declared Victoria.

"Besides, by entering into a joint venture with Cool Stuff, the Recreate Company is investing money in revitalizing Daisy's Square. When the work is done, there will be a sign to inform everyone that the area has been adopted and is taken care of by the two companies," Spender said proudly.

"And there's more to it!" Caroline added. "Mrs. Efficiency and her two co-workers are committed to giving recycling courses in poor communities. They will teach other people how to reuse materials by sewing and creating new products out of objects that would be discarded, like empty cans, soda plastic bottles and even used pens," concluded the girl.

"In Mrs. Constance's class, we've learned that everything can be re-created and turned into artwork or at least a useful object," Victoria informed the students.

Mr. Raymoney was delighted with the results of their work. When he was about to end the class, Money Boy raised his hand and asked to say something.

"I'd like to say that my mother is also starting her own business and our group is always committed to helping and suggesting ideas that comply with the three sustainability concepts: environmental, financial, and social," he said.

"Well, we've become curious now! Tell us about your mother's new business," Mr. Raymoney said, sounding interested.

"She is cooking and baking for her catering service. I'm also creating a website so she can sell online as well. It's a way to make some extra money and the coolest thing is that she loves cooking. The business is called Party House. Soon everyone will be able to visit the website. Please spread the word to your family and friends," Money Boy encouraged his classmates.

"That is news! I'm sure everybody here is going to help. After all, every new company needs to have its first customers to get started," stated the teacher.

Raymoney's last class ended in a party atmosphere. Everyone celebrated their successful work, the students were thrilled talking about it, and the holidays were just outside the school doors.

The girls surrounded Victoria and Caroline to talk about the diaries. The boys had suggested that the Recreate Company make small, square writing pads so they could use them as scorecards to register the soccer championship scores.

It was party time when all of a sudden the barking of a puppy outside made the students turn their heads toward the open door. The class became silent as they gazed at Nino running up and down the aisles between the desks.

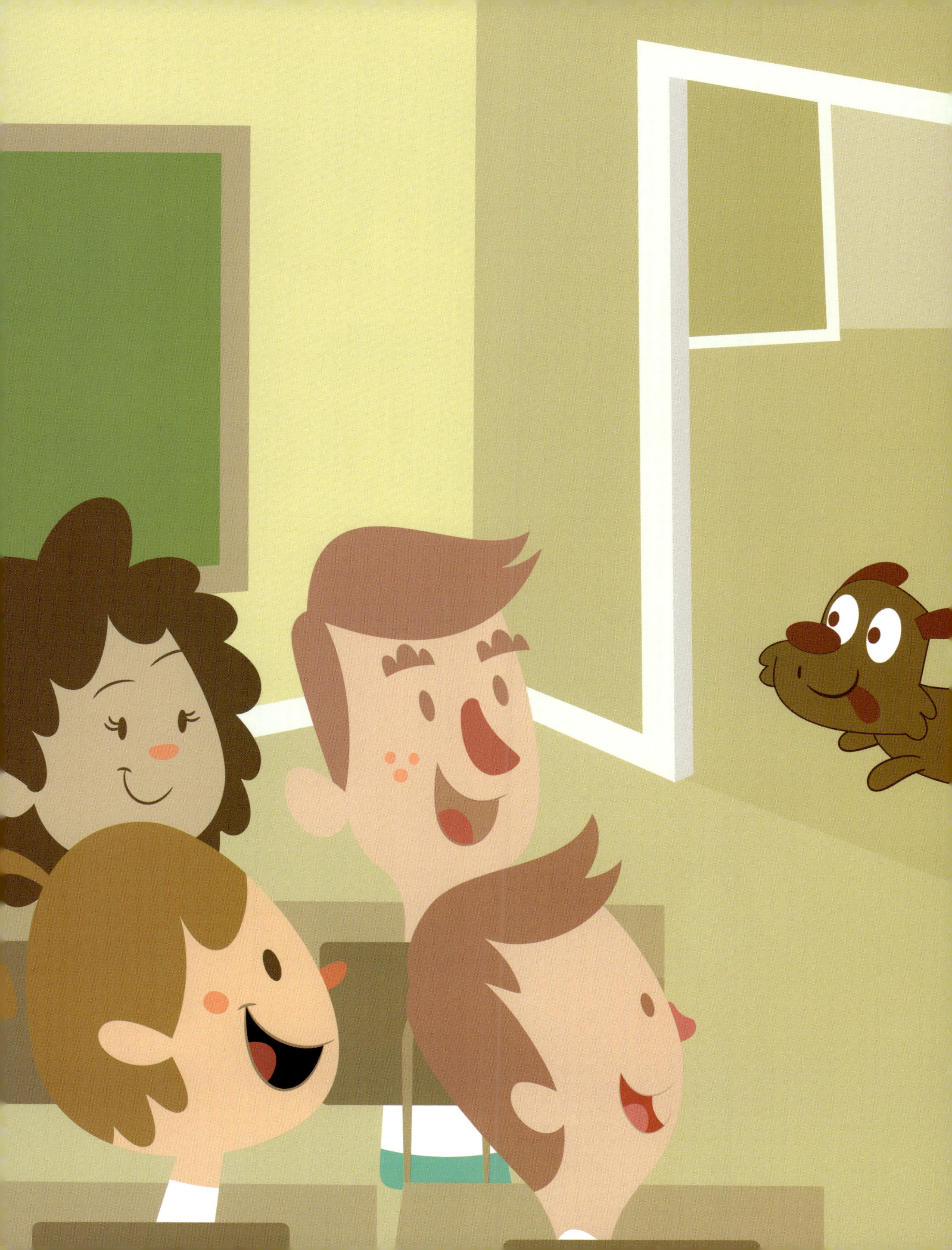

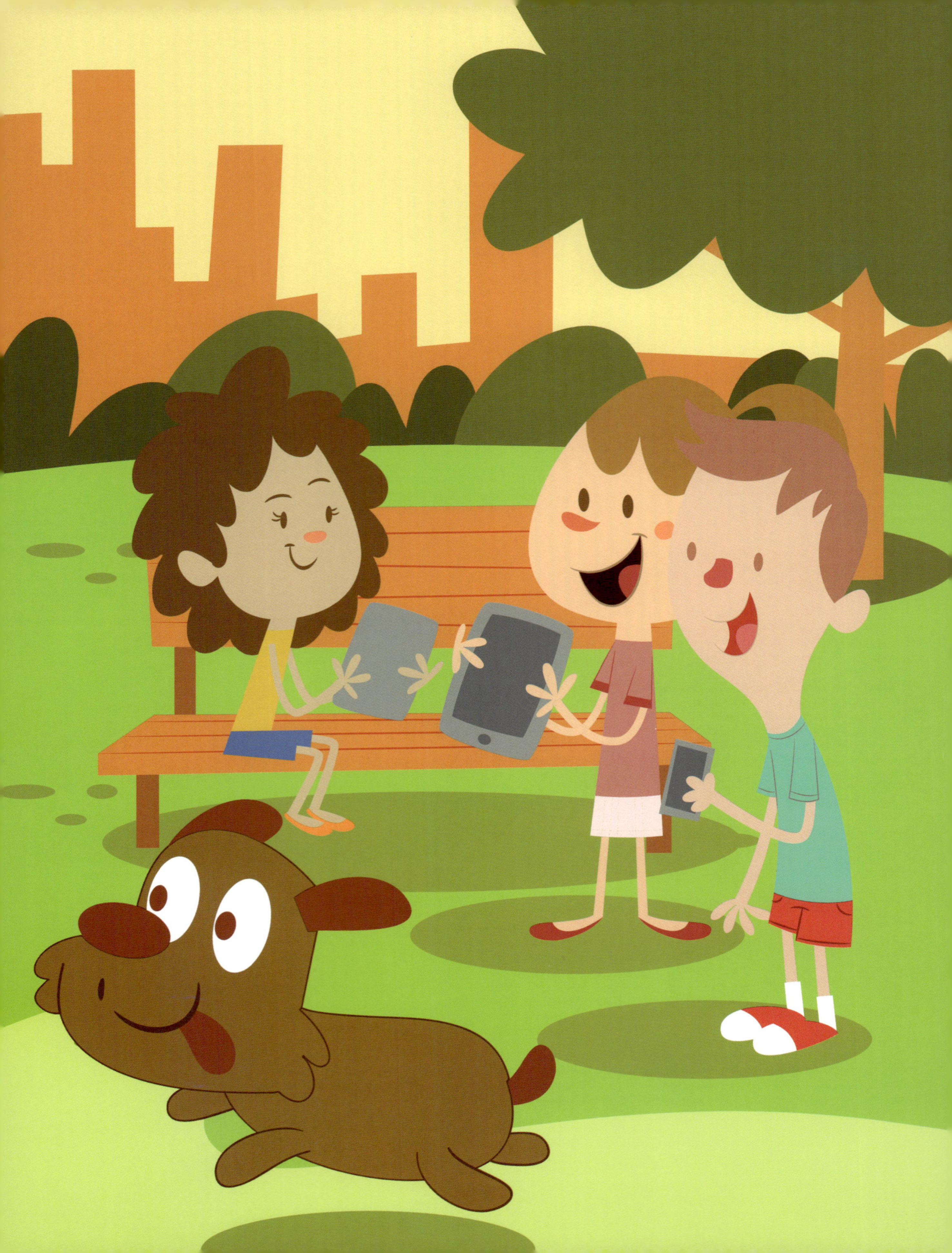

Celebrating at Daisy's Square

It was hard to imagine a dog coming into school without being noticed. Just behind him came Philip and Mary holding a piece of the leash that had broken off and set the dog free.

The teacher displaying a surprised look asked Money Boy what was going on.

The students were jumping out of their seats running after the dog. The puppy hid under the teacher's desk and sat down next to his feet. Money Boy explained to his classmates about Nino's Club and their rotation plan to give the puppy a home.

After listening to the story, several kids volunteered to take care of the dog. Nino's Club became a trend and everyone wanted to join it, even if it meant only having Nino every 15 days.

Mr. Raymoney remarked that it was a very good solution, but nobody quite understood what he meant. Most likely, they would have a lot more to learn in the next semester.

The kids and Nino headed to Daisy's Square. It had been completely revitalized after receiving financial support from Spender's father and his company, Cool Stuff, and from Victoria's mother and her company, Recreate.

Both companies supported the town's revitalization with money, but Daisy's Square also received major community support.

Everyone became involved and really worked hard so that within two months, the place became so beautiful that it turned into the town's newest postcard.

All the students celebrated the end of semester and Nino had fun with the kids at Daisy's Square.

Amidst the celebration, Victoria and Caroline sat under a tree, happy to be best friends. They showed each other their tablets and discussed how important the **DSOP Methodology** had been for them that semester.

With their tablets, they would be able to talk on the Internet during vacation and would not miss each other that much when they were away.

Money Boy came by and pulled a cell phone out of his pocket. The two friends were surprised and asked, "Is that yours?"

"Yes! It also surfs the Internet. It was my short-term dream for this semester. I saved some money and my grandmother gave me the rest as a gift, so I could buy it. Well, it's not new; it's a used phone. I paid a lot less than what the stores are charging for a new one."

"Wow, but it looks brand new!" Caroline stated.

"Yes, I think it was a good deal. Now I can be online, too, and will keep in touch with you, even during vacation," he said with a grin.

"Wow! That's great news. After all, you have your mother's company blog to take care of too, don't you?" Victoria remarked.

"Yes and you won't believe what happened!" said the boy, keeping everyone in suspense.

"What?" asked Caroline.

"Tell us! Tell us!" said Victoria impatiently.

"Annie's birthday is next month and she just told me her mother is calling my mom to order the birthday party kit," Money Boy said with eagerness.

"That's awesome! Party House's first customer. Congratulations!" Victoria said.

"Count on us if you need some extra help," offered Caroline.

"Thank you, girls! Thanks to our teachers and to what we've learned at school, we're able to suggest good ideas to our parents and help good things come true," the boy replied.

"Yes. Look at how beautiful this square has become. The daisies seem to talk to us!" said Caroline.

"That's true!" Victoria confirmed.

"How about your dad?" she asked Money Boy. "Has he managed to move to another department in his company? I remember you telling us something about it."

"Oh, yes! He took a course and the company's manager gave him a promotion. He even got a better salary," the boy said.

In the town of Lagoa Branca, the wind seemed to be blowing in favor of those who had fought for their ideas. The sun was shining in the sky giving off positive vibes for everyone living there.

In the joyful atmosphere that had surrounded Daisy's Square, Mrs. Sunday came closer to Nino. Even though the puppy hadn't met his new owner yet, he ran into her arms as if he already knew his fate had been decided.

In the end, everyone in the Square knew in their heart what it took to believe in the beauty of their dreams, even Nino, who finally found a new home to live in.

Author
Reinaldo Domingos

www.reinaldodomingos.com.br

Reinaldo Domingos is a master degree, professor, educator, and financial therapist. Author of the books: Financial Therapy; Allowance is not just about money; Get rid of debts; I deserve to have money; Money Boy—family dreams; Money Boy—goes to school; Money Boy—friends helping friends; Money Boy—in a sustainable world; Money Boy—little citizen; Money Boy—time for changes; The Boy and the Money; The Boy, the Money, and the Three Piggy Banks; The Boy, the Money, and the Anthopper; Being wealthy is not a secret; and the series Wealth is not a secret.

In 2009 he created Brazil's first textbook series of financial education aimed at grammar school, already in use by several schools in the country, both private and public. In 2012 he was a pioneer in creating the first financial education program for young apprentices. In 2013 that program also included young adults. In 2014 he created the first financial education course for entrepreneurs, followed by financial education as a university extension course.

Domingos graduated in Accounting and System Analysis. He is the founder of Confirp Accounting and Consulting and was the governor of Rotary International District 4610 (2009-2010). Currently, he is the CEO of DSOP Financial Education and DSOP Publishing. He is the mentor, founder and president of Abef (Brazilian Association of Financial Educators). He is also the creator of Brazil's first postgraduate course in Financial Education and Coaching and mentor of the **DSOP Methodology**.

Notes

Notes

Notes

dsop